Faith & LAW

A Practical Guide of Faith and
The Practice of Law

ANDREA HARVEY

www.selfpublishn30days.com

Published by *Self Publish -N- 30 Days*

Copyright 2018 Andrea M. Harvey Enterprises

All rights reserved worldwide. No part of this book may be reproduced or transmitted in any form or by any means electronic or mechanical, including photocopying, recording or by any information storage and retrieval system without written permission from Andrea M. Harvey or Andrea M. Harvey Enterprises.

Printed in the United States of America

ISBN: 978-1718693067

1. Family Law 2. Attorney

Andrea M. Harvey: Andrea M. Harvey Enterprises

Faith & Law

Disclaimer/Warning:

This book is intended for lecture and entertainment purposes only. The author or publisher does not guarantee that anyone following these steps will be a successful in faith or law. The author and publisher shall have neither liability responsibility to anyone with respect to any loss or damage cause, or alleged to be caused, directly or indirectly by the information contained in this book.

*This book is dedicated to anyone who
has ever wanted to give up on their dreams and said to themselves
I just need a sign to tell me that I should keep going:
This is it.*

Mission

The Mission of *Andrea Harvey Enterprises* is to inspire, inform, and motivate you to push through the difficulties of your situation and push through to your ultimate breakthrough and on the path to your purpose.

Acknowledgments

Wow. We are finally here. The book is finally here. And now it's my moment to give my thanks and appreciation.

First and foremost, as typical and expected as it may sound, I have to give honor to God. I promised God way back when if He would get me past "that" moment that I would never fail to give Him the glory for every moment after that. That moment has passed and many moments have come since then and I always stop to give honor where it is due first.

To my wonderful husband, Dionis. You picked me up off the floor in my darkest moment. You forced me to get off the couch and live again when I just wanted to give up and close the door on my dreams. Thank you for being there for me in my darkest hour and being there for me every hour since. I love you.

To my best friend, Ebony, who when I said to her, "Hey. I have a crazy idea. I want to open my own law firm." She responded with, "I don't think that's a crazy idea at all."

To Crystal, who answered the phone late one night around 2:00am the night before the bar exam and calmed my fears. You said to me, "No one has ever accomplished anything of significance in their life and when they were done said 'Whew! That was easy.'" I'll never forget that.

To my best friend, Kendre- who listens to me cry and makes me laugh instead. Who allows me to be Andrea/Drea/Attorney Harvey/A wife/and a sister friend all in the span of 20 minutes.

To Kurtis, one of my biggest cheerleaders. Who if I called him one day and said "Kurtis, I'm thinking of building a teepee on a mountain he would respond with, "What time are we meeting?"

To my dearly departed friend, Pete. I shared my dreams with you long ago. Before I was even old enough to make them happen. I never knew that you would not be physically here to see them come true, but that doesn't stop me from going after them anyway. I miss you my friend.

To Darren Palmer, my publisher, for pushing me. Pushing me. Pushing me. I'm a boss and I don't take too kindly to being bossed around. But you knew that already. Thank you.

To my mentors: Too many to name. Thank you for your wisdom and guidance over the years. It has been invaluable.

To my friends and family, for always giving me a reason to be proud and stand tall. Thank you for always being there.

Table of Contents

1. Introduction 1

2. Your Destiny Is In Your Hands 9

3. Trust The Source 23

4. Success Is Much More Than Just Money 31

5. The Timing Has To Be Right 39

6. The GPS Story 47

7. It's Not About You 53

8. Do Not Be Afraid 59

Conclusion 71

About The Author... 78

Chapter 1
INTRODUCTION

This book started out as a journal entry, or should I say journal entries. When I first started in practice, for months, I would journal day to day.

Venting, praying, crying, and working through issues. I just needed to clear my mind.

After a few years, I continued journaling and then I would often love to go back to my journal and see "where I was" mentally on that particular day. It was amazing to see the growth in real time.

As I began to look at past journal entries, I realized that I was unknowingly writing a *How to Run a Law Firm* book; however, it was a different kind of how to. A how to stay closer to God when all seems to be going in the wrong direction.

This book will help guide you how to:
- Lean into your faith when there's nothing else to lean on.
- Be a spiritual person in a none spiritual environment.
- Be a lawyer when you don't know what the heck you're doing.

All of that.

Business people are often cold and calculated. We don't care about who we hurt in the process, we just want to get it done. Sometimes we have to be. Sometimes there is no room for feelings. Especially when numbers are involved. Numbers and business are how we should see it.

However, regardless of how we want to reconcile the decisions we make, there is a spiritual nature in the work that we do. It's essential that we recognize that as early as possible in order to reach any measure of success.

Being in ~~private practice~~, working for yourself, is not easy.

Let me say it again: working for yourself is not easy.

Sure, there are certain perks (let me go ahead and get those out of the way early):

You get to make your own hours, you get to call the shots.

You get to decide when or where and how you will do something and there is no "man" telling you what to do.

With freedom, comes even more responsibility.

It's like that smug smile you get when someone asks to speak to whoever is in charge, and well, that person is you. As with anything, there is a downside.

No, that was not a book misprint. It was written purposefully.

For every upside in business, there is almost an equally weighing downside.

In other words, when things do not go well, you are 100% responsible. How simultaneously frightening/empowering! When I decided to go into private practice, it was not something I really wanted to do. I know

1. Introduction

that may come as a shock, but let me explain. My making the decision to go into private practice was me following God's instructions.

God does not do anything small; He does things big. Unexpectedly.

When He says move, I move.

Faith & Law

Notes

1. Introduction

Notes

Faith & Law

Notes

1. Introduction

Notes

Chapter 2

YOUR DESTINY IS IN YOUR HANDS

Commit your work to the Lord and your plans will be established.
—Proverbs 16:3

A few months before opening my law firm, I learned one of the most difficult and profound lessons of my entire career. One I will not soon forget - although the way I learned it came at the price of much pride. My life in Corporate America was one I cannot say I loved. If I was honest with myself, I joined Corporate America running away from the law. Yeah, that's it. I was running away from the law.

See, when I first moved to Chicago, I had difficulty passing the bar exam (more about that in another chapter). And because I had to get a job, I convinced myself that my next greatest career move was going to be in Corporate America. I wanted it. The corner office downtown in one of the tallest buildings in the Loop.

I settled for a cubicle in the middle of other cubicles in the suburbs of Chicago. I was on my way. I had been working for almost two years at a Fortune 500 company. My role within the organization was ad hoc at best. Management really did not know what to do with me.

They never said it, but I knew it. I was overqualified for a lot of roles. My education said that I should be a director or a leader somewhere, but my experience (and corporate politics) kept me "held down." My education and background required top dollar (I mean, it did). Despite my frequent demands, my company just was not in a position to pay me what I was worth. At least that's what I was told every time we did a review. So I continued to wait, work, and exceeded expectations. And do what I was told, when I was told or before I was told. Then one day, the opportunity of a lifetime came. Literally out of the blue.

I was sitting in my cubicle working diligently, and the Vice President of the company at the time personally came to my cubicle and said he wanted to speak to me. My first thought was, "Oh Lord, I am about to get laid off." I started calculating my severance package in my head and tried to remember if my resume was updated. I reasoned all of this while calmly walking to his oversized office.

Once we arrived, I saw that my Manager was present. Yeah, I was definitely getting laid off (in my head). Then my Manager saw my apprehension said, "Don't worry, you're not getting laid off!" (Was he a mind reader?) I relaxed a little and wondered the purpose of this impromptu meeting. I listened as the Vice President began to explain why I was in his office.

Apparently, my company had a brand new "top secret" initiative. This was something the company had never done. They needed someone to not only lead the program, but also design it from top to bottom. The person would not only be in charge of hiring, he or she would also be in charge of budgeting not only the program but

2. Your Destiny Is In Your Hands

the staffing for the program as well. He or she would be in charge of speaking to all outside vendors needed from a technological standpoint and infrastructure to support the program. This person was going to explain this exciting program to everyone in the company and make them excited about it. This person was going to design a million (or so) initiative to the President, the board, and all interested players. Yes. This person.

I was ecstatic! And honored. After I agreed to design the program, my manager and the VP gave me this comment with a nudge and wink, "This program when launched will need a manager, and naturally, the person who designed the program would likely be the manager of the program; so keep that in mind while you're building your team."

I did not inquire further, but I read between the lines. It was mine if I wanted it. I immediately got to work. Working on the new initiative, I had to work alongside a project manager. I learned a lot from her and quickly started doing some project management of my own. I had never done this heavy level of planning, but I loved breaking down processes to the smallest level and comparing that with what needed to be done on a larger scale.

My skill set was growing day by day. I was in meetings all of the time, and before long, because of my knowledge, I was leading meetings. I was spearheading conference calls, drafting plans, meeting with the outside vendors, sending out action items to other team members, and I even designed the website with the company's IT team. Yes, everything. I was doing all of this while I was also doing my other job.

Days became much longer and my workload basically tripled. I continued this juggling act for months on end. At first, I started out staying late, but after a few 7:00 pm nights, I would just work at the office then go home and work even harder. I became an avid reader and wanted to learn all I could about building a program of this kind.

I watched TedX talks and I eventually became what I would call a subject matter expert. Several more months of this building phase went, and little by little the program was ready for launch. Then the program launched. At the time that the program launched, the Director was not yet hired (nor were any of the supporting team members), therefore, I began to lead the program, support the program; oh yes, all of that while still also doing my former job. It was a lot. But I was convinced that my hard work would eventually pay off.

Finally, after a few months of this juggling act, the management team decided to move forward with hiring a Director for the program. Here I was thinking I was a shoe-in, but they told me I had to interview formally. How ironic that I had to submit my resume for a job description that I had actually written myself.

Not only did I go through an interview, I interviewed for several rounds. Each round of interview was with upper management. These interviews were interesting because they were all people that I had actually been meeting with to launch the program. I did not take that for granted, I still put my best foot forward and took it as I would a "Director style interview." I treated it as seriously. Still, no worries, no sweat. I had it! I put on my lucky suit, put on a brand new pair of stockings and some *bad* shoes!

All three rounds, at each level I breezed through the interview process. I confidently answered the questions and had real plans for making this program a success. Everyone seemed to enjoy my interviews and my vision for the future of the program. I thought I would hear

2. Your Destiny Is In Your Hands

something quickly. But that never happened. In fact, several more months went by without a word from anyone.

Oh, and did I mention that I was STILL running this program (while simultaneously doing my previous job)? All while receiving the same pay.

I would persistently follow up with my manager, and he would say, "They are still considering it, but you are definitely in the running for the leader." It was almost like a joke. Do you all want to see me work as hard as possible doing a job I'm not being paid to do just to see if I am willing to do it? I did not know. But I was tired.

Finally, after about two more months, my manager set up a meeting to discuss the program and my position. It was not a clouded meeting that was the actual title of the meeting.

Here we go.

I was going to hear about the changing of my roles. He spent the first few minutes telling me how great the program was running and how appreciative the company was for my hard work. We had some early success in numbers, and it was something to be proud of so "Thank you."

"You're welcome." (Now what about my job?)

After that, he let me know the news, I did not get the Director position. I was extremely upset, but tried my best not to show emotion. (I probably failed at that attempt.)

He told me that although I had not been selected to lead the program, I had been selected as a team member for the program (again, roles that I created). Ok.

I'm on the team. And then the gauntlet dropped "they have selected someone to lead the program and because I knew it like no one else I needed to train the manager." The same manager that I was going to work for.

Yes, you read it correctly, I was not hired to manage a program I designed, but I was being asked to join the team and train my manager to ensure their success in the program I designed. Also, no pay raise just a lateral move. So basically, I got a new title and a new manager who I had to train.

CRICKETS

Yes. This actually happened. If I'm lying, I'm flying. I promise I'm firmly planted in my seat as I write this. Yes, the same people who asked me to build the program and told me I would be a great leader asked me to train someone who would do a job I had been doing for months, and would ultimately be my manager. I had heard of this happening in Corporate America, you know those Corporate America urban legend tales, but I do not think I ever knew they were true. But yes, they were. And yes, they did happen. It happened to me. I was speechless; I am rarely ever speechless. I could do nothing but fake smile and contain my anger.

When I got home, I told my husband. He was naturally as upset as I was, but also pretty calm and asked what I was going to do. I had no response. I just wrapped up my thoughts and went to bed.

The next morning, I woke up and decided to call out of work. There was no way I was about to go to work in the mental state I was in. It wasn't embarrassment, I was honestly still shocked. I would have ended up more likely on the news for blowing up a building. So, that

2. Your Destiny Is In Your Hands

morning after sending the "I'm unable to come in today email," I sat at my computer and began to search for job.

I did not know much at that point, but I knew there was no way I could stay at that company long term. I had to go and the sooner I started this job search, the better off everyone would be. I started job searching as I had searched in the past but this time the search felt different. I was looking at legal jobs, and I was looking at corporate positions.

All over the place, the more I looked, the more depressed I became.

None of the jobs I saw were really listing anything I wanted to do. Here I was, a licensed attorney who had gotten her professional start in Corporate America. I was either extremely over qualified or under qualified for every single job that came up. Or looking at the job description, none of it matched what I wanted to do.

After a few hours of this search, I was so upset that I could do nothing but put my head down. I started to pray for clarity, and as I prayed, I heard the Holy Spirit speak to me. He told me very clearly and plainly to open my own law firm.

I was so shocked at the thought and message that I even looked up and said, "Who, me?"

And I heard just as clearly, "Yes, you."

I then said, "But God, I don't know what to do."

Then I heard Him say, "I do. Follow me."

I got up from my prayer, closed out the various search windows I had open, and immediately googled, "How to start a business plan?" The anxiety and dread that I had felt initially while job searching instantly went away. As I sat there, I became more self-confident and assured as I started writing out my mission for my life.

It was that day, from my living room table, that Harvey Law Office was born.

When you're growing up, you often hear the cliché phrase, "If it is to be, it is up to me." I heard that phrase most of my childhood/teenage years and even into adulthood. I never thought about the phrase very much, but at the same time, some kind of way, it always stuck with me. I'm not sure when I truly understood what that phrase meant, but I know that once I got that lesson, it was not one I would soon forget.

When going into business for yourself, you are the person that makes the decisions. Everything is on you. I didn't realize until later, all of those random skills I had learned in my previous positions would come into use. I have worked for companies of varying sizes.

One company I worked for was so large, we had a woman that had the sole position of planning and hosting events for the company. Yes, there was an in-house event planner.

When I first met her, I asked myself, "What type of company is this where we have someone in-house to plan events for the company?" It seemed like an important enough job and after working with her on several occasions, I came to appreciate her role. It was one of those background roles that made a big difference.

Going into business for myself, I quickly started to appreciate those people who handle those small but important tasks.

As glamorous as it seems, there will be days when you spend your entire day handling more business than the actual practice of law.

Or more days that you spend being an IT Specialist rather than a lawyer.

Or an accountant.

2. YOUR DESTINY IS IN YOUR HANDS

Or an administrative assistant.

There have been days that I have been on the phone with AT&T because my internet has gone down for no reason at all. If I can't get on the internet, I cannot work; if I cannot work, then I'm not making money — and when I'm not making money, I'm losing money.

You are responsible for the decisions. You and you alone. Become very comfortable with the idea that you are in charge of your destiny. The instant you are upset because of situations beyond your control, you are taken off of that path.

For example, as I type this chapter, I am sitting in the middle of Whole Foods. The internet at my house is out because there was a storm and power is out everywhere, the internet at my office was going in and out because of the same storm. I was initially aggravated - downright pissed, to be honest. But I had to step back and assess the situation.

I am in charge of my destiny.

I determine how my day goes.

Sure, I have no control over the weather, but nothing is stopping me from relocating my person (and my computer/and limited files) to a place that can meet most of my basic office needs. And that place just happens to be Whole Foods. But you get my point. You have a choice, and it's up to you to make the best decision for you and your business.

Your destiny is in your hands.

Faith & Law

Notes

2. Your Destiny Is In Your Hands

Notes

FAITH & LAW

Notes

2. Your Destiny Is In Your Hands

Notes

Chapter 3
TRUST THE SOURCE

As I mentioned in the introduction of this book, I opened my law firm based on an instruction from the Holy Spirit. I wish I could tell you that after that day, I started to seek Him for all of my decisions, but that is not the case. Usually, I will go at something on my own, bump my head several times and then after realizing it's not working, end up going right back where I should have started in the first place.

The first day I was officially open for business, I sat at my kitchen table (I didn't even have a desk then), turned on my computer, and then looked around the room and waited for the magic to happen. For a good five minutes or better, I just sat there and took in the enormity of the moment.

I had my own law firm now - ok... now I had to do something with it. Then I looked down at my phone. No, it wasn't ringing (yet). I had to work to make that phone ring.

So, I got to work. And work. And more work. And... more work.

I opened my firm in April and had my first client by May. It was a relief. Ok. I was officially in business, and this wasn't a hobby or something I said- I had a client.

Can I just tell a secret? When I first started, I just wanted a client. Not ten clients, not 20 clients, just one person. One person who would trust me enough to take their case. My desperation was written all over my face, actions, and attitude. I was practically begging at the door for them to sign on.

Now, I have finally reached a place in my practice where I can turn down clients. When you first open, you're just happy someone is there and willing to pay. You're happy the phone rang, and the person was actually calling to speak to you and not trying to sell you something.

At that point, a paying client is a good client. Later, you learn that a paying client isn't necessarily a good client and just because your phone rings doesn't mean you:

1. Always have to answer it.
2. Always have to accept what's on the other end.

Yes, some clients will pay you on time and top dollar. But there are others who will pay you little to nothing and expect top dollar service. You learn fairly quickly that taking anything that comes in the door will make you regret the day you signed on as their attorney. Regrettably, it can cost you so much more none monetarily in the end.

As I became more and more experienced and confident for that matter, I began to go to God about every one of my clients. I trust His judgment much more than mine. Before they walk in the door and after they walk out of the door, I pray for them and for me. During their case,

3. TRUST THE SOURCE

as I'm filing motions and going to court, I pray. I pray so I can hear from my Source.

Almost anyone has had the feeling before a case starts, "This client is not a good client for me or they are going to be annoying...."

Somehow, we still sign on with them. Why? Let's just keep it real, it's because we need the money.

But let's unpack that for a minute; who is your source? The clients or God? If we are to trust Him in everything, wouldn't we also trust that we will be ok? That even in our lowest moments financially He will still provide?

So, I've talked about the source, but do you know the Source? Can you hear His voice?

What does it sound like to you? It's not the same for everyone, but I can assure you the commonality is this: the source is that voice inside of you that speaks to us all through the day. It's a voice that's speaking not loudly, but in a gentle whisper. It's the same voice that we cannot hear when we are speaking above it or too chaotic in our minds to even hear it.

Trusting the source is not just with clients, it is with other business people. I did not go to law school in the city in which I practice. Actually, I'm not from the city I practice, did not grow up in the city where I practice, and believe it or not when I moved here knew only one person (my now husband). Needless to say, networking was a must for me. When I go out and meet people, it has been an experience all it's own. I have met my fair share of personalities, to say the least.

Some people take themselves too seriously, some do not mean you any good, some are just trying to get your number, some are mean, but there are others who are genuinely good people. To tell you the truth, the "just plain old good people" are few and far between.

But, I would rather have a solid 10 good people than 100 that do me no good.

I have allowed God to lead me to the right people organically. I do my best not to force meetings and situations. It's ok if someone reschedules with me a million times and never makes good on the meeting. It's ok if I go to dinner with someone one time and I never hear from them again. I do not take it personally when I call someone and they do not call me back. Sure they may be busy, but ultimately, I allow the Source to insert (and remove) the necessary people in and out of my life.

Having said that, my practice and my network for that matter is unique, but it works for me. All of my friends are not attorneys. In fact, I have more none attorney friends than attorney friends. I do not only go to law firm networking events, I go to other business types networking events. These events have yielded me much more business success anyway.

My method of trusting the Source and allowing Him to organically create my network and clients has proven to be a long process, but it's a beautiful quilt that works for me. They all do not look like me, are not all in the same profession as me, but we share a kindred spirit that connects us above any superficial traits. For my clients, I know that my skill set is perfect for their needs (and if it doesn't work, I do not force it to work). No rhyme or reason to it, it just is.

I cannot impress upon you enough the importance of looking to the Source to guide you as you begin to establish yourself as a professional in your chosen field.

3. Trust The Source

Notes

Faith & Law

Notes

3. Trust The Source

Notes

Notes

Chapter 4
SUCCESS IS MUCH MORE THAN JUST MONEY

Let's face it. If you open a business for yourself, you are hoping that the business makes money. You can call it what you want, but if you did not go into business to make money, you would have started a not for profit. If you start a business, your goal is to make money with that business. Period! Now, it may not be at the top of your list, but it's somewhere in your mind.

When you got started, if you're anything like me, you probably even have a business plan with a fancy graph with financial projections. I will fully admit I had the same projections, but the reality is those are projections only. Projections with possibilities but projections do not always turn into money.

Here is another secret: my first year in business, my finances came in much lower than I had projected. Ok. Much lower than I had expected.

Yet, I still feel in some ways I was successful. I'll explain more.

I did a consultation with a potential client once. He was coming to me after firing his previous attorneys. He was now moving on to what would be his third set of attorneys, which was red flag number one. After speaking to him in more detail, I ended up declining representation. During our consultation, he said something that really stuck out to me - he was upset because his previous counsel had charged him over $50,000 in legal fees, and after all that time and money, the case was still not completed. $50,000.00 and two attorneys later, the case was still going.

Ok, I tend to get caught up in the minutia but seriously when he told me that he had spent over $50,000 in two years on two attorneys, that gave me pause. Serious pause. Up until that point, I thought that I was doing pretty "good" as an attorney. I paid my bills mostly on time, and every once in a while had a little extra to treat myself (or my law firm) with something shiny and cool. However, when he quoted that figure to me, I thought to myself, "I am clearly doing it all wrong." Not getting into specifics but that's a lot of dang money to make from one client and one case.

After that call, I started to feel bad and wonder if I was even doing a good job as an attorney. I am not here to judge those attorneys; they may have earned that large bill. But it was my internal comparison to them that taught me the lesson of 'defining success.'

When you are in business, you will learn very quickly there is a spectrum of incomes for business people. People are out here faking the fancy as I like to call it, meanwhile they are one client away from losing it. Trust me, I know because I've been there. But I've also been on the upside of it as well; more clients than I know what to do with and more money than I've ever seen. But that's not my point. There are some business people out here doing well, and there are others doing ok, and then there are some barely making it. I will not say where I am,

4. Success Is Much More Than Just Money

but I can assure you I am not (YET) making $50,000 off one client and one case.

I was watching Oprah's Life Class one day, and Iyanla Vanzant said something that really stuck with me. She said (and I am paraphrasing) that being jealous of another person's success is disrespecting the God in you. That hit me to my core. I realized there had been times in my private practice life that I had been outright jealous of other attorneys. Seriously, I will look at what I think they are doing and have a full on "why not me" tantrum in my head. I would look at them and look at me. Look back at them and look back at me. And the more I looked at them and back at myself, I repeatedly decreased my own true value.

Sometimes, I would even question whether or not I should continue in practice. I (in my head) was nowhere as smart as them, as well off financially as them, and definitely they knew more, so what was I even doing calling myself "having my own law firm?" There were times when I would literally say to myself, "Who do you think you are?"

All of those negative talks would circle around and around in my head and if I listened long enough, I would start to believe it. If that ever happens to you (and no matter how confident we are in ourselves it can happen), STOP IT! That type of thinking is not only detrimental to your day and your self-image, it's also harmful to your goal.

You're on a mission. You don't have time to define your success by someone else's standards.

As a person in charge of your destiny, you ultimately make the decisions. You create the benchmarks, you create success- it's YOU. If you are ever upset about what has "not" been done, you should be angry with yourself. Not them, you. When you engage in this negative self talk, you're essentially saying to God, "You must have stopped blessing people when you left their address. I guess you have forgotten about me." You should know that the same God that gave to them can give to you. The same God that blessed them can bless you. Besides all of that, you do not know what they had to go through to get those things.

They may have had sleepless nights, lost family members, lost friends, lost money and even lost their mind. Are you willing to make those same sacrifices to get what "they" have?

There may be things you may not be so willing to go through even if given a choice.

Define your success for you and work within those ranges. Your success will reach you where you place it. When it is time to grow, you will. And remember, success has levels. There are days when the most successful thing I have accomplished is returning all emails and voicemails, clearing out my inbox and finishing what was on my to-do list for that day. Yeah, you may not win them all, but at least you did not set an impossibly high bar for yourself and then internalize the failure when you do not reach it. Your initial measure of success may be to maintain five clients at a time. Or maybe even one client at a time. You define it. And when you reach it, raise the bar.

4. Success Is Much More Than Just Money

Notes

Notes

4. Success Is Much More Than Just Money

Notes

Faith & Law

Notes

Chapter 5

THE TIMING HAS TO BE RIGHT

In previous chapters, I spoke about receiving the direction to go into private practice. What I didn't say is that I worked almost six months at my previous company before leaving to open my own practice. I knew God wanted me to open my firm, but I also knew that He would tell me when it was actually time to open my firm. And of course, He did. A few months after my business plan was complete and I had socked enough savings away, I woke up and knew it was going to be the day I quit my job. No fan fair or anything, no special singing of the birds, and no, the heavens did not open, but I had a peace about it that I cannot explain.

The day I was going to give my two weeks' notice, I worked that day as usual. I didn't go in flipping tables and stealing office supplies from the supply room. I did not stand on the tables and tell everyone I was out and drop the mic (let me have my fantasy moment, ok?). I got off at my usual time. When I came home, I sent my boss my two weeks' notice. It was fairly straight, and to the point.

It stated the following:

Good evening,

After much thought and reflection, I have concluded that it is the best professional decision that I end my working relationship with [insert company name].

This email shall serve as my two-week notice. My last day will be April 15th.

Thank you for your time, and I wish you all the best in the company's future endeavors.

After several years my two weeks notice amounted to four sentences.

When I got to work the next day, shocked and surprised would describe their faces. My manager had the biggest "deer in headlights look" I had ever seen. Remember, I had trained her in her new job. She was still heavily dependent on me, but I knew it was time for her to flourish on her own. Yes, this was the same manager that I was training to have 'my' job, perhaps she did take it from me.

Maybe she was a part of the corporate game of chess of which I happened to be the pawn, but that did not affect how I would treat her.

In fact, I was pleasant, helpful, and as friendly as I could be. Not once did I ever blame her for taking "my" job nor during my transition did I keep things from her. At the same time, I had given her all I had to give, and it was time for me to move on. I was so happy that day.

I was dancing to my own beat, finally.

When you're in business for yourself, you must learn to dance on beat. I do not mean that literally, but figuratively. Even if you can't dance, you have to keep pace with your life and know the right time to

5. The Timing Has To Be Right

do anything: when to roll out a certain initiative, when to introduce a marketing plan: everything happens in its own time.

When we do things out of order, it is only going to do nothing but slow us down. For example, when you are dancing, you can only clap or dance on beat once you catch the rhythm. Some people take a while, others even longer, but keeping proper timing is something you either learn to do or forced to do.

My greatest example of this is the day I had to appear in court for a fellow attorney. I had agreed to a ridiculously low amount for coverage out of town. I was doing a favor for a friend of a friend. He wanted me to go to another county to make an appearance in court.

He would pay me upon my return. I didn't have a car at the time, so I had to get a zip car (trust me, financially I was losing before I got started), drove almost two hours to this county only to be told once I had arrived it was the wrong time and date.

Talk about upset. Here I was breaking my neck for someone else, and they had given me wrong information, so I thought.

I drove to Starbucks, got a coffee and sat down to type him an angry/professional email.

He was about to GET IT! Let me tell you how my day had started: I had missed the bus because I had to go back to my house to get an umbrella because it was raining. When I went to get my rental car, it wasn't available at the time, and I had to go to another location.

I get to the other location, and the car didn't have any gas in it. I had to stop and put gas in the car. On the way to court I was caught in a traffic jam due to construction and to make matters worse, it was raining heavily. I went through hell and high water (in real life) to make it to a court date only to be told I was there on the wrong day.

When this first happened, I thought, "It's ok. It's just a day. It happens."

So, when I opened my email to type this attorney an angry "who do you think I am" email, I got the surprise of my life. Hours earlier the night before, the attorney had sent an email with the updated correct date and time, the email apologized for the mix-up and wanted to make sure I got the email before I got up on "that morning" to go to court.

Here I was, too caught up in my own drama that I had neglected to do the one thing that would have corrected this entire issue - stop and think. See what happens when we move too fast?

We are so busy forcing life to happen that we do not realize it's happening all around us. Learn to dance on beat.

5. The Timing Has To Be Right

Notes

Faith & Law

Notes

5. The Timing Has To Be Right

Notes

Notes

Chapter 6

THE GPS STORY

I love my husband, not only because he is my husband, but sometimes he says some of the most profound things unintentionally. One day, I was explaining (read: complaining) to him about how I felt as if I hadn't heard the voice of God in a while.

I was so upset because as I explained earlier, I had heard God tell me to open my firm. He had been clear about that. I had also heard Him when He told me it was time to leave my job. I had heard Him in those moments when I had to turn down or accept clients, but for some reason, I wasn't hearing Him on what I was to do "next."

I felt he had been silent for a while and I really did not know what to do next. Has that ever happened? When you're praying and praying… and praying and still, it's as if you only hear radio silence.

I explained this to my husband, and he said to me the simplest thing, which I will share with you here. It is a pretty short story, and it really bears no explanation.

When you set a destination into the GPS as you first start driving, it gives you step by step directions. The GPS knows where you are from the satellites and it will start to guide you where you need to go. Even out of your own neighborhood you will hear it tell you turn left, turn right, stop at a stop sign, and it will sometimes even tell you which expressway to take and how far away it is from your current position.

But once you're on that expressway and especially if you're on it for some length of time, the GPS will go silent. In fact, anything over about ten miles or more, the GPS will only show you and tell you how long you will be on that particular expressway. But what the GPS will not do is ask you to keep going.

Even if you're on a stretch of highway for thirty miles, every mile, it will not say, "Keep going straight." You'll just look at your screen and see a line that keeps going as far as the screen will see.

Isn't God a lot like that? At the beginning, He may give us step by step instructions, tell us to go left go right, but once we are on a straight path, it's not necessary for Him to constantly say, "Keep going," or sometimes He will not even tell us how far we have to go.

Continue to trust that when it's time to turn, your time to exit, and if there is a slow down up ahead, He will speak and direct you accordingly.

6. The GPS Story

Notes

Faith & Law

Notes

6. The GPS Story

Notes

Faith & Law

Notes

Chapter 7
IT'S NOT ABOUT YOU

We've all seen them; law firms named, "Last Name, Last Name, and Last Name." Or "Last Name and Associates." I always chuckle at those names. Shoot, my law firm is named after me. And let's face it, there is a certain level of pride that comes when you have your name hanging from a shingle. The first time my name was above my law firm name on a name tag at an event, the nerd in me gave myself a high five and fist pound. I was so proud of it - I kept that name tag and put it on my wall.

It's ok to be proud of your accomplishments, but always remember that it is never about you. I am often asked how I can do this or able to do that, and most of the time I hesitate to answer. Not because it's a hard question to answer, but because I do not have an explanation for it.

There are times when I am in court speaking, and it is nothing but the Holy Spirit working in me. Sure I have some legal knowledge, but the words? That's God.

I have had professional opportunities fall in my lap in such a way that my only explanation is prayer and belief. I wish it could be deeper than that, but it's not. After this happened a few times, I quickly began to realize that God truly works in mysterious ways.

It's interesting now because I have always shied away from ministry. My father is a minister, and I just have a "thing" against that whole 'first family' mentality. Having grown up under the watchful eye of an entire church body (at least that's how it felt) I longed for the days where I could be a pew warmer. I know that seems so contradictory to my personality, but it is the truth.

However, God makes the calls in my life. Whereas I would never call myself a minister, I do understand that I have a voice for His message. I am always happy to share it any way that I can, in any method I can.

Practicing law can get ugly. Particularly family law. There are high stakes and emotions from clients and attorneys. Whereas the work I do (family law) does not necessarily yield winners and losers, there will still be someone at the end who did not get the outcome they envisioned. That is inevitable.

No matter what profession you are in, there is always a way to let God's light shine through you.

This book isn't for everyone. It's for those who are praying to hear these exact words.

To that woman or man who is reading this, know that it's not me, but all God.

Allow Him to speak to you, through you, and watch and see what He can do in your life.

7. It's Not About You

Notes

Notes

7. It's Not About You

Notes

Notes

Chapter 8
DO NOT BE AFRAID

"So do not fear, for I am with you; do not be dismayed, for I am your God. I will strengthen you and help you; I will uphold my righteous hand."
—**Isaiah: 41:10**

If this is your first time reading the verse, read it again. This verse is basically telling us, do not be afraid. When I first opened my practice, where there was a part of me that wanted people to know that I was open for business, there was also a part of me that wanted it to be a secret.

After I was open for a few months, a friend of mine bluntly said to me (Shout out to Raijean Stroud, Rest in Peace, baby), "How are people to know you are in business if you do not tell them?"

She forced me to ask myself that day, "What exactly was I afraid of?"

Sometimes in business, we will face situations and occurrences that are out of our skill set. Sorry to spill the beans to the readers, but no, you do not graduate from law school knowing every single thing there is to know about the law.

We graduate from law school with the basics; just enough to know how to go out and learn every single thing there is to know about the law. But even still, that is no reason to fear!

God is with you every step of the way. There have been times when I was banging my head against my desk and heard the voice of God tell me to call someone. This person was the exact person I needed to talk to that could talk me through the legal issues and help me sort through it. Do not be afraid to even make that call. If you have gotten your network of people, then your network is the type that will not judge you when you call them.

I once heard, "Continue to work at it until it doesn't frighten you anymore."

What does that mean? Learn. Learn some more. And when you think you've learned it all, learn even more. You cannot ever stop learning or growing. You only get better with time.

I know I've talked a lot about spiritual principles and being a business owner. But a business is still a business and there are certain business concepts I have to teach you about it. I wanted to give you a few tips that are practical and helpful that can help you in business (faith filled or otherwise):

A. ROBBING PETER TO PAY PAUL

You've heard it before. The statement that you're robbing Peter to pay Paul. It's inevitable, a client will call you at 7:30 p.m. on a Tuesday night before a major hearing at court, they do not have an attorney, found you online, and want to hire you.

But there's just one problem - they don't have any money to pay you "right now," but on Friday, they can pay you. So, what do you do?

8. Do Not Be Afraid

Take the case? Give them a rain check? No. You do none of the sort. You give them your retainer and your price. If they can't pay it, that's ok. You had no plans to go to court anyway. Good day to them. And if they really want your services, they will come up with the money. Trust me, they come up with it.

This is simple enough but be clear; I do not work until you pay me. I have learned that someone that does not have the money today will not have the money tomorrow. Particularly those that call you and need you immediately. Absolutely not. You're asking for an entire attorney's work with a portion of their pay? No. No way. No how. Not then. Not ever.

There was a time when I worked with people and gave them the benefit of the doubt, but I realized that there was no way to give everyone a rain check and survive on "I owe you" receipts.

If you treat paying your bill like an option, people will treat it the same way.

I hate to sound ugly, but it's the truth. You have electricity, rent/mortgage, water bill, gas for your car and whatever else you need to survive. You are able to pay that because people pay you.

When people don't pay you, the money doesn't magically appear. Stand firm on your prices and stand firm on your payments.

B. BRANDING

When I was in the planning phases of my business, one of the first things I knew I wanted before I even had a physical location was an online presence. In this day and age, people almost judge the legitimacy of a business off of their website and social media presence.

In order to have a webpage, it made perfect sense for me to have a logo. I needed to find that one symbol that people recognized about my business before they even recognized me.

Want to know how logos and phrasings work? Think about your latest visit to the store to pick up some necessities. Your brand of body soap - did you have to search for long to find it? Did you even read the label? Or did you just look at the price and remember what the container usually looks like? Or perhaps you were trying a different brand this time, what did you compare? The price and how much was offered? Most people do.

Our businesses are the same way. Think of it this way, when you go into business for yourself, you are lining yourself up on the shelf with every other person that offers the same thing.

Perhaps you're the first of your kind and that way, when someone looks for your services, you'll be the only box on the aisle that offers what you offer. Which if that is the case, this chapter still applies to you.

Or maybe you're like every other business, sure you offer different services, but you fit into the same category of services. So, you have to ask yourself a few questions.

What is it about my business that stands out from the other companies like mine?

What do I offer? What is it about my business? That is your brand.

If you knew nothing about the inside of the brands behind the label and was just making a decision based on a need, what are you going to choose? One of the first things people look for is price. As a business, you have to know what your pricing will be. How much is the

8. Do Not Be Afraid

value of the services you offer? Why is your price at this rate and what does your price entail?

I'm not asking for a deep analysis on market trends and the current climate of the economy (although this is on a small scale what you are doing), I'm asking you how much are you worth? It's all a choice but a smart choice to make.

If someone was selling a house for say $20, you would know automatically that something was wrong with that house. Why? Because things of that value are not usually priced that cheaply. Same thing about your brand.

When people come to you, you are establishing and presenting your brand. What are the services that you are offering that are going to be so good that someone will choose you as opposed to the next person? What will make them remember you? However, your brand should not only be recognizable, but it has to be sustainable.

I'll give an example that I think most people can understand. Back from the 1990s, to say about 2005 or so, Blockbuster promoted themselves as the "what to do on the weekends" alternative. Everywhere you looked, you saw Blockbuster this and Blockbuster that. Their prices were moderate. They even sold popcorn and drinks in the building. One stop shopping. Blockbuster was so successful, they were popping up on every corner, in every city. A few smaller companies even mimicked their business model and were able to duplicate their own level of success.

Then came a little company named for exactly how it looks, "Redbox." It introduced the even cheaper, no employees to deal with, you choose on your own "drive through" movie concept. Everywhere you looked suddenly there was a Redbox on every corner or in the parking lots of your frequently visited locations.

Next thing you know, there came another company Netflix. At first, you paid for a subscription and could see as many movies as you wanted in a month for one price, and then they elevated to streaming services. Little by little, you saw less and less Blockbusters until eventually, they went out of business completely. A large company could not compete with a little Redbox and the convenience of streaming online.

Sure there are other streaming companies, but you get my point. The brand was built, and it did not evolve with the time and eventually failed.

Now Netflix is not only a video rental company, it's a production company and even apart of the culture- 'Netflix and Chill' anyone?

So I ask, "What is your brand going to do to sustain the test of time?" A business cannot just be built off of the people. If it was only built on the people, there wouldn't be any more Walmart stores or Sam's (shout out to Sam Walton and the Walton family).

Your brand has to last the changes of times. You can change it at a moment's notice, don't get stuck trying to hold on to old concepts in a modern society. Make sure when you're building a brand, it's not just built on your shoulders. If you go away, then so does the business.

Let me just say that maybe you are building a business totally dependent on you, and that's ok. But also realize that a brand dependent on its founder and cannot exist beyond the founder. When the founder goes away, so does the business.

8. Do Not Be Afraid

A brand dependent on its concepts can last as long as its concepts last. As long as the services are needed, the brand can sustain. A brand can only be one of two things: either dependent on its founder(s) or dependent on its concepts. But even if it's dependent on its concepts, be prepared to change with the times.

Faith & Law

Notes

8. Do Not Be Afraid

Notes

Faith & Law

Notes

8. Do Not Be Afraid

Notes

CONCLUSION

I cannot believe that I'm telling this story, but somebody somewhere needs to hear this. I did not pass the bar exam the first time. Nope, I did not. There is a genuine, practical reason that I graduated almost three years before actually practicing law.

Now, on my biography, the gap is hardly noticeable. But in real life, there is a reason for that gap. I also want to tell you that I passed the bar the second time but if I did tell you that, I would be lying. And as much as I want to say loudly, I passed the bar the third time because everyone knows that it is a charm, I cannot say that either. What I can say, because it is the truth is that it took me four times to pass the Illinois bar exam. Whew! Ok. There. I said it.

You may have just read that quickly, but it has taken me years to say that out loud. But I said it. I do not share this because I am proud of it. I am not. In fact, for me, it is one of the most embarrassing things I have ever admitted to myself out loud, and much worse, in print.

I wish I could tell you why I knew God wanted me to take that awful exam as many times as I did. I still do not know. I can tell you the story of my quest to climb over the wall of that exam and how I finally reached it. I believe and trust this story will help you as much as it did me.

When I graduated from law school, I like many of my fellow law school graduates across the nation had high hopes. I was going to graduate on a Saturday and two months later on the last Tuesday and Wednesday in July take the test that would walk me right into practicing law.

A big firm job was sure to come, and the big check would not be that far behind. In my estimation, by the fall of that year, I would have my passing results, a job I went to every day from 9 am-6 pm, a bank account full of money.

Oh… and I would proudly discuss all of this over the Thanksgiving table. Yeah, I had it planned out pretty well.

However, things did not come that easy to me when I first took the bar exam.

In fact, the day I went to sit down and take that first part, I knew and felt it in my spirit; this was a mistake. I sat there and those questions may as well have been in another language. That's how much sense they made to me. I had never been so underprepared in all of my life. Seriously. I thought I knew so much, but I feel like that exam tested me on every single thing I did not know.

I walked out of that test and went straight home and cried. I knew I had failed, but people assured me. 'No, everyone felt like they have failed/I'm sure you did better than you think you did. No one ever feels they knocked it out of the park, etc.' I heard it all.

When the results came out, I was devastated. So devastated, in fact, I laid on the floor for about two days straight. At first, I was devastated, then, I was also assured. Hey… it happens. Not everyone passes the first time. Not even all of my law school classmates had passed the

CONCLUSION

first time. So I did not feel completely alone. I was now a member of the "repeater" club. While it is nothing to be proud about, there are members of the club, so you do not feel so alone.

Repeaters are a different breed of bar takers. We know the test but have natural confidence issues. So, when I took the bar the second time, I was surprised that I had no confidence issues.

That fall, I had studied until I couldn't study anymore. I reached a new level in my studying. I would study from 7:00 am until 8-9:00 pm. Six days per week. I did this for two months straight.

Listen, I knew what I knew, knew what I didn't know, and knew what I didn't know so well that I could pretend as if I knew it. So when I walked out of the exam after the second day, I was confident but still a little nervous. Sure, it was a gamble. But I had done my best. I felt good about my performance.

The results came in the spring (by the way, I took the bar exam on my birthday that year, how lucky could I get?) I opened the letter and once again, I was "unsuccessful." This time, it really hurt. I missed passing by five points. 1-2-3-4-5. I had failed to pass the Illinois Bar Exam by five freaking points.

So now, at that point, I was downright embarrassed. Where I was embarrassed before, people are ok with you not passing the first time, but the second time, it gets kind of shameful. You leave the "repeater" club and join the "multiple repeater club." That club is even smaller, and the members are more secretive and people much less forgiving.

At this point, most of the people I took the test with the second time had passed this time around. So I did not have a pity party squad, I just shut down for a few days. No phone calls or emails. I had to reset.

Two times and still no passing score? Maybe practicing law wasn't for me. I had tried and failed twice, that was enough for anyone's ego to know when to fold them.

Maybe this was God's way of telling me, "Hey you tried, and that's good enough for me." But somewhere, somehow deep down, I knew that wasn't the case. I was so tired of studying and having that cloud of "the bar exam over me," I decided not to take the bar exam the next go-round. I would take the test when I took it. Who cared at that point?

One day, out of the blue it seemed, I got an email. It was a reminder that my Professional Responsibility Test scores were only good for so many more years. I needed my scores to still be good so I needed to pass the bar exam within the next year. "Ok. Whatever," I said. I'll sign up when I sign up. No big deal, I still had time. Weeks passed, and I still had not made up my mind.

One night, in the middle of the night, out of nowhere I heard this noise. It was a RINGING in my ear. Loudly. I woke up and looked around. My dog was sleeping soundly, my husband was sleeping soundly, surely they had heard this noise. Why was this noise so loud? Ok, maybe I had only heard it. I tried to go back to sleep convinced I was having a weird dream. Tossed and turned. And just as I was falling asleep again, the ringing began again. I got out of the bed, looked out through the window to see the source of the noise and saw nothing.

I walked into my living room and said out loud, "Ok God, what are you trying to tell me?" He replied instantly in my spirit, "Register and take the bar exam." Yeah, I was tripping. I know God did not tell me to do that. So I went back and got in the bed. Next thing I know, the ringing began again.

Conclusion

Finally, I got up, went to my computer and the page was already up for the Bar Exam registry. There was a red notice on the page; it stated that the next day at 12:00 pm was the absolute last time to register for the upcoming exam.

So I completed the registration that night, looked online for a place where I could mail my application and have it overnighted to the board of bar examiners, and placed it in an envelope prepared to pay the next day – express delivery. After the envelope was sealed, I instantly got sleepy and went back to bed soundly. It was the oddest thing. As I was preparing my application, it was as if I was in a trance. Sometime was guiding me to complete those tasks to get my application mailed. After I put it away, I instantly got sleepy. At that point the ringing had stopped and I went straight to bed.

The above story is so crazy; I have never told anyone about that until now. So here I was, registered to take the bar exam, for now, a third time. And in my mind, I thought if God told me to take this exam, I had gotten up in the middle of the night due to a ringing in my ear, I just KNEW that time I would pass it.

A few weeks later, studying began. I studied… and studied. This time was even more different from the first two times. It was a breeze. I was studying full time and working full time. I would work all day then study all night. I would be off on the weekends and study all weekend. I did not have much of a social life, sleep was a commodity I could not afford, but it was a sacrifice.

This time, when I took the exam, I felt even more confident than both times before. God told me to take the exam, so I was a shoe-in, right? Imagine my surprise when the results came two months later and once again, I was unsuccessful. You guys. I was unsuccessful by three points. 1-2-3.

Devastated does not begin to even tell you how I felt. Embarrassed, who cares? Wasted time, who cares? Sleepy, who cares? I was angry. I was hurt. And I told God just how I felt in my usual way- rejection.

I stopped praying. I stopped journaling. I could not even bear to speak to God. I was not hiding. I did not know what to say without any of the words starting with "why me again?" After a week or so of this, I finally had to tell Him how I felt. How dare He tell me to do something and then not give me the results I wanted. I had woken up in the middle of the night, filled out the application, and sent it in overnight shipping. I had studied and worked, and I had sacrificed so much - was that not enough? What more did He want me to do?!

It took a while, but I calmed down. I was speaking to a good friend and telling her how upset I was. I had done what God told me to do, and I felt cheated. She then said to me something I would never forget. She told me, "Just because you do what God wants you to do does not mean that He is going to give you what you want. It was never about whether you passed or didn't pass. It was about your obedience." "Wow," was all I could say in response.

How true was that statement? How many times in your life have you followed the voice of God, followed His instructions to the letter only to feel like you did not get the results that you wanted? I am here to tell you it is not about you getting what you wanted, it is about your obedience.

Well, I am happy to report as you have probably figured out that I did take and pass the bar exam on the 4th try. This time was a little different from the others. This time I walked in with confidence and

CONCLUSION

walked out and said aloud, "Lord, have your way." I had never said that before. The entire time it was about me getting what I worked for. That last time? That last time was different. I was not worried about the results. Not at all.

I went into that test knowing several things:
1. That test did not define me.
2. God was greater than any test I had ever taken, passed or failed.
3. Whether I passed that test or not, I had given it the best I could get, and God had done the rest.

Finally, and most importantly, it was never really about "the test." It was never about me studying. It was never about my results no matter how far away they were. This was about obedience, and not allowing a test (or the results of that test for that matter) to define who I was.

God's timing is always perfect, and I could not have crafted a perfect story myself. I did not tell this story to brag or even have you pity me. I want to tell you that we all have some things in life we have to overcome to reach our goals. It is in our overcoming that truly builds our muscle and defines the type of business people and people in life we will ultimately be.

*Now answer this for me, are you ready to
walk in faith and the law? Let's go.*

FAITH & LAW

CONCLUSION

ABOUT THE AUTHOR

Andrea Harvey is a true Georgia peach and has lived in Chicago since 2007. Since she was in the 4th grade, Andrea has definitively said "I want to be a lawyer." Always at the top of her class throughout school, Andrea was able to get a scholarship and attend Mercer University in Macon, Georgia where she obtained a Bachelor of Arts degree. Andrea then moved to Fayetteville, Arkansas to attend law school where she graduated from the University of Arkansas School of Law.

Upon her graduation, she moved in Chicago, Illinois to immediately begin her legal career. Finding difficulty in passing the Illinois bar exam, Andrea initially gave up her dream of being a lawyer and began to climb the corporate ladder. Despite finding success in corporate America, her childhood desire to finish what she had started would never go away. Eventually, Andrea triumphed and passed the Illinois bar exam. Inspired to follow her dreams, Andrea left her role in the corporate environment and opened her own law firm, Harvey Law Office.

Since opening her own law firm, Andrea has received many awards including: Top 40 Under 40; Top 100 Lawyers; 10 Best in Client Satisfaction just to name a few.

Andrea is a Certified Mediator. She is also licensed to practice law in the State of Illinois and licensed to practice in the Federal Courts of Illinois.

In addition to running her own law practice, Andrea enjoys sharing her legal knowledge related to family law with the community. Her podcast and video series, Harvey Law Speaks, serves as a platform for Andrea to answer frequently asked legal questions and help people understand their legal rights in the area of family law.

Passionate about motivating others, Andrea serves as a guest speaker at various events where she encourages young people and professionals to go after their goals and pursue their purpose. Andrea also speaks at events where she educates women and men about their legal rights within the field of family law.

Andrea resides in Chicago with her husband and two dogs. In her spare time she enjoys visiting with her family and friends; traveling; reading and gardening.

Conclusion

Made in the USA
Columbia, SC
04 July 2018